DESERT

Veronica Bonar

HEINEMANN

A ZOË BOOK

Devised and produced by
Zoë Books Limited
15 Worthy Lane
Winchester
Hampshire SO23 7AB

First published in Great Britain in 1992 by Heinemann Educational Books Ltd., Halley Court, Jordan Hill, Oxford OX2 8EJ

OXFORD LONDON EDINBURGH
MADRID PARIS ATHENS BOLOGNA
MELBOURNE SYDNEY AUCKLAND SINGAPORE
TOKYO IBADAN NAIROBI GABORONE HARARE
PORTSMOUTH NH(USA)

ISBN 0 431 00182 0

A CIP catalogue record for this book is available from the British Library.

Printed in Italy
Design: Jan Sterling, Sterling Associates
Picture research: Alison Renwick
Illustrator (cover): Cecilia Fitzsimons
Production: Grahame Griffiths

Photographic acknowledgments
The publishers wish to acknowledge, with thanks, the following photographic sources:

t = top *b* = bottom
Cover: J Allan Cash Photo Library; Title page: J & D Bartlett/Bruce Coleman Ltd; pp6 Anthony Bannister/NHPA; 7 Jan Griffiths/Robert Harding Picture Library; 8 Anthony Bannister/NHPA; 9*t* Gerald Cubitt/Bruce Coleman Ltd; 9*b* John Shaw/NHPA; 10*t* John Visser / Bruce Coleman Ltd; 10*b* Gerald Cubitt / Bruce Coleman Ltd; 11 M Fogden/Bruce Coleman Ltd; 12 Nigel Dennis / NHPA; 13*t*, 13*b* Anthony Bannister / NHPA; 14*t* Ashod Papazian / NHPA; 14*b* Michael Leech / NHPA; 15 Leonard Lee Rue / Bruce Coleman Ltd; 16*t* Anthony Bannister / NHPA; 16*b* Wilkins / Bruce Coleman Ltd; 17 G Ziesler / Bruce Coleman Ltd; 18t Rod Williams/Bruce Coleman Ltd;18b Peter Johnson/NHPA;19 Gerald Lacz / NHPA; 20, 21*t*, 21*b*, 22, 23*t* Anthony Bannister / NHPA; 23*b*, 24 Jane Burton / Bruce Coleman Ltd; 25t Anthony Bannister / NHPA; 25*b* Norman Myers / Bruce Coleman Ltd; 26 Peter Ward / Bruce Coleman Ltd; 27*t* J Meech / NHPA; 27*b* Nigel Dennis / NHPA.

Title page
An ostrich can run at nearly 65 kilometres an hour.

Contents

This is the desert	6
Desert plants	8
The flowering desert	10
The search for water	12
Saving water	14
Daytime in the desert	16
Keeping cool	18
Moving across the desert	20
Under the desert floor	22
Desert nightlife	24
Food in the desert	26
Glossary	28
Index	30

This is the desert

Very little rain falls in a desert. The sun and the wind soon dry up any water or early morning dew on the surface of the land.

In some deserts, the wind blows the sand up into hills or **dunes**. The loose sand piles up on one side of a dune, and rolls down the other side.

▲ Desert soil is mostly too dry for plants to grow. At an oasis the underground water is at or near the surface. The long, deep roots of palm trees reach down through the soil to the water.

Desert winds blow from different directions. They make the dunes move and change shape. Some dunes have high, steep sides. They may be more than 300 kilometres long and up to 200 metres high.

The desert floor is usually a mixture of sand, stones and bare rock. In some places, there is water at or near the surface of the land. These places are called **oases**.

Desert plants

It is difficult for plants to live in dry places. Desert plants often store water in their stems or roots. Some plants have a waxy coating on their leaves. This helps to prevent the water in the leaves from drying out, or **evaporating**, in the hot sun. Some plants have very small leaves so very little water evaporates, while other plants have no leaves at all.

▶ Naras plants grow on the sandy desert floor. The plant has sharp thorns and tiny leaves. Its long roots find underground water. The prickly naras melons are full of pulp and seeds. They provide food for desert animals such as the oryx, ostrich and fennec fox.

◀ Acacia trees have small leaves and long roots which grow down nearly 30 metres into the soil to find water. This acacia tree provides shelter for the termite nest beside it. The nest may have more than one million insects inside it.

Some desert plants have wide, shallow roots near the surface of the soil. The roots spread out to catch any dew or rainfall. Other plants have long, deep roots which reach down to underground water.

Many desert plants have sharp thorns or prickly stems to prevent animals from eating them. Other plants grow and flower only when it rains. If there is no rainfall, they remain as fruits or seeds, lying on the dry desert floor.

▼ Euphorbia trees have branching stems, and prickly spines instead of leaves. Their stems store water in the form of a juice. Animals do not like the taste of this juice, and will not eat the trees.

The flowering desert

Sudden thunderstorms or a heavy shower of rain will bring the desert to life. Dry, yellowing plants grow green again and start to flower. The dry seeds take in the rain-water, and new plants develop and grow rapidly. The plants spread over the ground, soaking up or **absorbing** water from every small pool of rain. Within three days the desert floor is a carpet of flowers.

▲ Some euphorbias are small, low-growing shrubs. They look like cactus plants. The flowers grow at the tips of their spiny stems.

▶ A sudden shower of rain has left pools of water on the desert floor. The shrubs and plants burst into life. Birds and insects feed on the pollen and nectar of the flowers. They carry the pollen from one plant to another.

◀ Desert flowers bloom for a very short time. Butterflies, moths, wasps and bees help to pollinate the flowers. These insects, together with their eggs, provide food for spiders, scorpions and many birds and reptiles.

Most desert plants live for only about 10 or 15 days before the moisture disappears. The plants stay alive long enough to flower and produce seeds, but the seeds may have to wait for a year or more before it rains again.

With so little rain, desert plants need to scatter their seeds as far as possible to catch any showers. The seeds of some desert grasses have spiky hooks which catch in the fur of passing animals. The wind blows away the dry seed cases of other plants. Sometimes the wind uproots plants and blows them into new areas of the desert, where they may grow again.

The search for water

Desert animals, birds and insects spend more time looking for water, than they spend looking for food. Many larger animals, such as oryx, may travel a long way every day to drink from one of the few water-holes. Then the animals return to their grazing grounds, where dry grass and small bushes grow.

▼ An oryx drinks at a desert water-hole.

◀ Sand grouse live in large flocks. When a cock bird finds water he first drinks for himself. Then he paddles in the pool and soaks his belly feathers in the water. The feathers absorb water like a sponge. When the feathers are as wet as possible, the bird flies back to the nest. The chicks crowd around him and suck the water from his feathers.

▼ Desert ants drink from a droplet of water. Scientists think that the fine white hairs on the ants' backs help to keep the ants cool.

A few animals, such as the fennec fox and the addax antelope, never drink at all. Fennec foxes take in liquid from the insects, plants, lizards and **rodents** that they eat. Addax antelopes and Dorcas gazelle get enough liquid from the juice, or **sap**, in the leaves of plants. Kangaroo rats, gerbils and jerboas use the moisture stored in seeds.

Falcons and larks take in liquid from the insects they eat. Other seed-eating birds often have to travel long distances from their nests to find water. Sand grouse fly several hundred kilometres to drink. They also carry water back to their chicks in the nest.

Saving water

▲ The long-eared desert hedgehog lives in burrows during the day to keep cool. It comes out at night to catch insects.

Desert animals have different ways of saving water. The temperature on the surface of the dunes during the day can be over 65°C, but beneath the surface, the sand is much cooler. Many desert insects and small animals burrow into the sand to escape from the heat. The animals do not sweat in the cool underground burrows, and so their bodies lose less water. They stay in their burrows all day long.

The droppings of desert animals are very dry, and the animals pass very little water in their **urine**.

▶ Prickly pears store water in their stems. The stems have a waterproof, waxy coating to prevent evaporation. Instead of leaves, this plant grows spines, which stop animals from eating it. The stems do the work of leaves and make food for the plant.

Larger desert animals, such as oryx, camels and antelope, cannot hide in burrows. Gazelles, antelope and oryx have shiny coats which **reflect** the heat away from their bodies.

Camels have a thick, woolly hide which protects, or **insulates**, them from the rays of the sun. The thick fur slows down evaporation when the camel sweats. The camel's long legs keep its body away from the scorching desert floor.

▲ A camel can go for up to ten days without drinking or eating. It lives on the fat which it stores in its hump. The camel feeds on bushes and dry grass. It can drink 130 litres of water in ten minutes.

Daytime in the desert

▲ Oryx graze at night when the plants have more dew on them. During the mating season, male oryx use their long horns to fight other males.

▶ Dung beetles eat and collect animal droppings. They roll the dung into a ball. The beetles make a hole in the ground for the ball. The female beetle then lays an egg in the dung.

Although most small animals stay out of the sun during the day, many spiders and beetles do come out to feed. Their hard outer skin stops them from losing water by evaporation.

Lizards run across the burning sands, hunting these animals. At night, when the temperature in the desert falls rapidly, the lizard's body gets cold. In the morning, the lizards warm their bodies in the sun. They can control their body temperature only by moving out of the sun into the shadow of rocks or stones. Lizards and snakes are **cold-blooded animals**.

◀ Unlike other birds, owls hunt at night and spend the day resting in trees or cracks in rocks. The owls eat insects, reptiles, birds and even small deer. An eagle owl's pale, sandy feathers help it to hide among the sand and rocks of the desert.

Most desert birds hunt for insects and other food during the day. They usually shelter in shady places during the midday heat.

Many desert birds, such as the desert lark, have sandy-coloured feathers. The colour makes the birds hard to see against the desert floor. This type of protective colouring is called **camouflage**.

Keeping cool

▲ Dabb lizards are about 35 centimetres long. Their strong tails are covered with hard plates for protection. Dabb lizards change their colour according to their surroundings. They burrow into the sand in the hottest part of the day.

Desert animals have different ways to keep cool. Larger animals shelter in the shade of a rock or a tree. Even lizards cannot stay in the midday sun too long, so they shelter in holes or under rocks.

Ground squirrels come out of their burrows from time to time during the day. A ground squirrel spreads out its bushy tail over its head and back to shade its body from the Sun. After about fifteen minutes the squirrel returns to its burrow. It presses its belly against the walls of the tunnel to cool down.

▶ Springboks take shelter in the shade of an acacia tree. Acacias stay green all year round. Camels and other animals graze on the tender acacia leaves, in spite of the tree's long thorns.

Some animals pant to cool down. Panting draws air into the moist lining of the animal's mouth. The saliva evaporates and cools the blood in the tissues underneath.

Birds pant by fluttering their throats. This makes a current of air pass across the moist inside of their mouths. Their thick feathers help to insulate their bodies against the heat.

▲ The huge ears of a fennec fox help to cool its body. The tiny blood vessels in the ears are very close to the surface of the skin. Air blowing across the fennec's ears cools the blood which flows through these blood vessels.

Moving over the desert

Moving across the hot, loose sand of the dunes is very difficult. The feet of many desert animals have grown in special shapes, or **adapted**, to help them to keep a foothold on the hot, slippery sand. Camels have broad, spreading toes that prevent them from sinking into the sand.

▼ A sidewinder viper moves across the sand by rolling its body sideways in a series of S-loops. It makes a set of tracks in the sand as it moves.

◀ A chameleon runs carefully on tiptoe across the hot tarmac of a desert road. The grasshopper on its back is hitching a lift! As the chameleon runs, it holds its body well clear of the hot road surface. Its long tail helps it to keep its balance.

Fringe-toed lizards have a fringe of scales on their feet. Some kinds of lizards, such as geckoes, have **webbed** feet. Webs and fringes prevent the animals from sinking in the sand and are useful for digging. Sand lizards shuffle their feet as they walk. They push aside the hot surface sand to uncover the cooler sand beneath.

Some types of skink do not use their legs to walk. They hold their legs close to their bodies, and wriggle through the sand as if they were swimming.

Gerbils, jerboas and kangaroo rats leap over the sand's shifting surface. Gerbils have tufts of hair on their feet which give them a good grip on the sand. The hair may also insulate their feet from the hot surface.

▼ Like most desert spiders, the wandering spider does not spin a web. It digs into the sand or hides in a crack in the rocks. Its long, thin legs help it to move easily over loose sand. Desert spiders hunt at night or at dusk to avoid the heat of the day.

Under the desert floor

Many desert animals hide under the sand or in burrows to keep out of the sun. Fennec foxes dig a deep burrow about one metre below the surface of the sand. Here the temperature is cool and the fennec foxes can sleep through the day.

The desert viper buries itself in loose sand to cool down. Only its eyes show as it lies in wait for birds and rodents.

▶ Geckoes leave their burrows at night to catch scorpions, spiders, centipedes and insects. The hair-like fringes around this gecko's feet spread the animal's weight. It can skim over the surface easily, without disturbing the sand.

◀ Wolf spiders hunt by day. Their huge eyes look out for their prey. They chase after their victim and pounce on it. Wolf spiders live in holes in the ground which they close with a trapdoor. The female carries her newly hatched spiderlings on her back for safety.

▼ Mole rats live most of their lives underground, in the long tunnels that they dig. Their wrinkled pink skin has no fur. Mole rats have tiny eyes and long front teeth. They live on the water which is stored in the underground roots of plants.

Jerboas seal off their short tunnels with a thin wall of sand to keep out the hot air. The air inside the jerboa's burrow gets damp as the animal breathes. When it breathes in, the cool air absorbs the unwanted heat in the jerboa's lungs. When it breathes out, the warm air touches the jerboa's cool nose. The air turns into moisture, or **condenses**, forming a liquid which the jerboa can lick off.

The jerboa is often attacked by snakes inside its burrow. It builds two entrances and can escape from either one when danger threatens.

Desert nightlife

▶ When gerbils leave their burrows, they stand up on their hind legs to look around. If they sense danger, they beat on the ground with their hind legs, or make shrill cries, before they quickly disappear back down their burrows.

When night falls in the desert the temperature drops quickly, and the heavy dew makes the ground damp. Scorpions, spiders and centipedes come out from their holes or from under stones to hunt for insects. Geckoes run across the cooling rocks, looking for beetles and other insects to eat. Small rodents leave their burrows to search for seeds or insects.

Gerbils and jerboas need to be very quick to escape from larger animals such as the fennec fox or jackal. These animals would kill the smaller ones. They are called **predators**.

A jerboa looks like a small kangaroo. It has short front legs, long powerful hind legs and a long tail. A jerboa can jump three metres off the ground, and change direction in mid-air to escape from danger. If an enemy comes too close the jerboa throws sand in its face.

▲ A dune spider leaves the shelter of its burrow to hunt for insects to eat. Desert spiders have a thin layer of wax covering their skin. This layer prevents the spider's body from losing water by evaporation.

◀ This scorpion has caught a caterpillar. Desert scorpions come out only at night. They do not see well, and hunt by smell and touch. A scorpion grabs its prey with its claws. It kills its victim by injecting poison through the sting at the end of its curved tail.

Food in the desert

Plants are an important source of food for many animals. Some desert animals, such as gazelle and oryx, eat only plants. They are **herbivores**. Many other animals eat a mixture of food, including plants. In order to survive, the plants produce far more seeds than is necessary. Seeds also provide food for desert insects, birds and rodents.

Many insects **breed** only when the plants are in flower. Some of these insects live for a very short time, but they leave behind a large number of eggs and **larvae**. These are an important food supply for other insects, birds, snakes and lizards.

▶ This robber-fly has caught a butterfly. Robber-flies hunt every kind of flying insect. They inject a liquid into the body of their prey. The liquid breaks down muscle tissue so that the victim cannot move.

◀ Desert lizards run very quickly over the sand. They stand with their heads held high. The lizard pushes on its front legs so that it lifts its body clear of the hot sand.

▼ Falcons hunt soon after dawn. They have excellent eye sight. They catch their prey with their claws, and tear it apart with their hooked beaks. After feeding, they soar in the cooler air high above the desert floor.

Rodents such as gerbils and mole rats also feed on the plants. These animals are eaten by the birds, snakes and desert foxes. Lizards and scorpions eat spiders, beetles and other insects. Birds of prey keep a sharp look out for these animals on the desert floor.

Desert animals, like desert plants, have to be tough. Some animals can live without food for many days. Darkling beetles can survive for more than 130 days without eating. These beetles have a layer of air between their bodies and their wing covers. The air insulates the beetles from the heat.

Glossary

absorb: to take in water.

adapt: to change something so that it becomes more useful.

breed: to mate and, in the case of insects, to lay eggs and larvae from which new insects will develop.

camouflage: the colouring of the fur, feathers or skin, or the shape of an animal, that makes it hard to see against its background.

cold-blooded animals: animals that cannot make heat to warm their bodies.

condense: to change from water vapour or steam into drops of water.

dune: a hill of sand.

evaporation: when water turns into water vapour in the air.

herbivore: an animal that eats plants.

insulate: to prevent heat passing into or out of something.

larvae:	the second stage in the life of insects, after the eggs have hatched out.
oasis:	a place in a desert where plants grow because water is there.
predator:	any animal that kills another animal for food.
reflect:	when heat or light bounces back off the surface of something.
rodent:	an animal, such as a mouse or a rat, which has long front teeth, used for gnawing.
sap:	water and minerals that are carried from the roots of a tree to its branches and leaves.
urine:	the yellowish coloured liquid that takes waste materials away from the kidneys in the body.
webbed:	with a skin between the toes.

Index

acacia 9, 18
addax 13
animals 8, 9, 11-16, 18-23 , 25-27
antelope 13, 15
ants 13
bees 11
beetles 16, 24, 27
birds 10-13, 17,19 ,22, 26, 27
burrows 14, 18, 22-24
bushes 12, 15
butterflies 11 ,26
camels 15, 18, 20
caterpillar 25
centipedes 22, 24
chameleon 21
cold-blooded animals 16
Dabb lizards 18
darkling beetles 27
deer 17
desert hedgehog 14
desert lark 13,17
desert viper 22
dew 6, 9, 16, 24
Dorcas gazelle 13
droppings 14
dune spider 25
dunes 6, 7, 14, 20
dung beetles 16
eagle owl 17
euphorbia 9, 10
evaporation 8, 14-16, 19,25
falcons 13, 27
fennec fox 8, 13, 19, 22, 25
flowers 10, 11
fringe-toed lizards 21
gazelles 15,26
geckoes 21, 22, s24
gerbils 13, 21, 24,25, 27
grass 11, 12, 15
grasshopper 21
ground squirrels 18
herbivores 26
insects 9-14, 17, 22, 24-27
jackal 25
jerboas 13, 21, 23, 25
kangaroo rats 13, 21
larks 13, 17
larvae 26
leaves 8, 9, 13, 14, 18
lizards 13, 16, 18, 26 ,27
mole rats 23, 27
moths 11
Naras plants 8
nectar 10
oasis 7
oryx 8, 12, 15, 16, 26
ostrich 8
owls 17
palm trees 7
panting 19
plants 7-11 ,13, 16, 26, 27
pollen 10
predators 25
prickly pears 14
rain 6, 9-11
reptiles 11, 17
robber-fly 26
rodents 13, 22 ,24, 26, 27
roots 7-9, 23
sand 6-8, 13, 14, 16-18, 20-23, 27
sand grouse 13
sand lizards 21
scorpions 11, 22, 24, 25, 27
seeds 8-11, 13, 24, 26
shrubs 10
sidewinder viper 20
skinks 21
snakes 16,23,26,27
soil 7,9
spiders 11, 16, 21, 22, 24, 25, 27
springbok 18
stems 8-10, 14
sun 6, 8, 15, 16, 18
sweating 14, 15
termites 9
thorns 8, 9, 18
urine 14
wandering spider 21
wasps 11
water 7-10, 12-16
water-hole 12
webbed 21
wind 6, 7, 11
wolf spiders 23